The Star-Man
and Other Tales

Basil H. Johnston

Jonas George *(Wah-sa-ghe-zik)*

Illustrated by
Ken Syrette *(Nohdin)*

ROM
Royal Ontario Museum

© 1997 Royal Ontario Museum

All rights reserved. No part of this publication may be reproduced, stored in a retrieval system or data base, or transmitted in any form or by any means, electronic, mechanical, photocopying, or otherwise, without the prior written permission of the publishers.

First published in 1997 by the Royal Ontario Museum,
100 Queen's Park, Toronto, Ontario M5S 2C6

Managing Editor: Glen Ellis
Designer: Virginia Morin

Canadian Cataloguing in Publication Data

Johnston, Basil, 1929-
　　The star-man and other tales
ISBN 0-88854-419-7

1. Ojibwa Indians - Folklore. I. George, Jonas.
II. Royal Ontario Museum. III. Title.

E99.C6J594 1996　398.2'089'97　C96-931347-0

Printed and bound in Canada by Friesen Printers

Contents

Thunderbolt *(Nimkiiwaagan)*

9

Short Tail *(Tukwaunowae)*

13

"Dog! Bring Me a Beaver!" *("Animoosh! Amik Abeedimoowishin!")*

21

Mermaids *(Nebaunaubaequaen)*

27

Thunderbirds *(Nimkii-Bineshiinyag)*

33

Thunder/Monsters *(Nim-Mah-Kie/Miisaandamoog)*

39

What the Dog Did *(Animoosh w'gauh izhitchigaet)*

43

The Closed-Eyes Dance *(Pizungowaubigauh)*

53

The Star-Man *(Nangiiwnini)*

59

Introduction

The ancient storytelling and picture-making traditions of the Ojibway people find contemporary expression in the retellings of the myths and legends by the elders and in the illustrative interpretation of these tales by Ojibway artists.

As the artists are the successors to their ancestors who painted, often in ochre, on rock and hide, so the storytellers are a continuous line reaching deep into a spiritual past. In their honour, the Royal Ontario Museum is pleased to bring together stories told by present-day narrators Basil Johnston, Sam Ozawamik, and Frank Shawbedees with others told by Jonas George *(Wah-sa-ghe-zik)* early this century, all of the tales illustrated by Ken Syrette *(Nohdin)*, of the Batchewana First Nation.

Imbued with humour, wisdom, and mystery, the tales and the art reveal the continuity and power of the Ojibway myth-making tradition.

Anishinaubaek is an Ojibway word having various translations—"the people" and "the good beings" among them. It is the name that many Ojibway now prefer to call themselves. The singular form, and the adjective, is Anishinaubae, which is also the language of the Anishinaubae people. These words are often spelled Anishnawbek, Anishnawbe. The pronunciation is usually (a)nish-NAH-bek, (a)nish-NAH-bay.

The publishers wish to thank Harvey Anderson (*Nimkie-Benishie-Nini,* "The Thunderbird Man"), elder of the Chippewa of Rama, for his guidance in the interpretation of Rama stories told by Jonas George (*Wah-sa-ghe-zik,* "A Shining Day"), which were collected by Colonel G. E. Laidlaw and first appeared in the *Ontario Archaeological Report* of 1914 and 1916. Thanks also to Amy Alison, of the Curve Lake First Nation, a teacher of the Anishinaubae language, who generously advised regarding the translation of legend titles for "Thunderbolt," "Thunderbirds," "Monsters," and "The Star-Man."

Thunderbolt

Nimkiiwaagan

Told by Jonas George *(Wah-sa-ghe-zik)*

Rama First Nation, 1914

Many years ago, a young man went out to hunt early one morning, and coming on noon he got hungry and started back to camp. In passing a pine stub that had been struck by lightning, he saw something sticking in the tree where the lightning hit. He pulled it out and looked at it. It was about two fingers broad, and about one hand long. He put it back again in the tree exactly as he found it, and went on.

When he came to camp he told his father about it, and his father and several other men, together with the young man, went back to examine it. Neither his father nor the men could remove it, but the young man could; so he pulled it out, wrapped it up, and took it to camp.

Whatever this was, it would tell the people some hours before a storm came up that the storm was coming, so that they could make camp. The young man used to dream that he could split trees by pointing it at them, but he never tried it. He kept it for many years. It was lost shortly before he died. He died unmarried and his name was forgotten.

It was shiny and quivering, and nobody knew what it was made of. No one knew what to call it; no one could make up a name for it.

Short Tail

Tukwaunowae

Told by Basil H. Johnston

Translated from the Anishinaubae by Basil H. Johnston

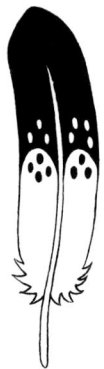
The bear awoke one spring, and off he went. As luck would have it, he met a fox. Apparently, this fox was dragging a string of fish.

"Where did you get them?"

"Oh, in the lake; you too ought to fish."

"Isn't it plain that I do not have a hook?"

"Just put your tail into the water. You will not believe how many fish will be sticking to it."

Anxious to catch fish, the old bear set out across the ice. Then he made a hole in it and set his tail down into the water. He sat there all night. In the morning, it is said, he yanked his tail out of there. Believing that there must be a huge number of fish attached to it, he yanked his tail suddenly. They say that he went sliding along the ice. But soon he started to sense something around the area of his posterior, as if in fact bees were stinging him.

When he turned to look, he saw that there were no fish. There was also no tail. So he went back to take a look at the hole in the ice. He saw his tail there. It was weaving, they say, very much as a river meanders. However, there were no fish.

Only then did he at last realize that he had been tricked by the fox. So he went out in search of him.

All during the spring he sought out that fox.

Then, one afternoon, he saw him in the distance, running along a ridge. At this opportunity, the bear hailed him. "Alright, fox. I'm looking for you. I will catch you, you can be sure. And when I do, I'll kill you for what you did to me."

"Ha! You wouldn't catch me," the fox taunted.

"It would actually be better," replied the bear, "if we were to fight tomorrow. I'll meet you here."

"Agreed," replied the fox.

"Feel free to bring your friends also," noted the bear. "For myself, I will be alone."

"You should be the one looking to bring friends," remarked the fox. "If you have any, that is."

The bear was enraged by the fox's words. Like that, he was gone. The fox left at the same time.

Soon, the fox met a lynx. "Excuse me," he said. "Are you a good fighter?"

"Am I a good fighter? That's all I do; it's unbelievable how well I fight."

"How do you fight? Show me."

Instantly, this lynx made off for a deer. He killed it without any difficulty. He gored it and he tore it. "That is how I fight," he said.

"The bear is going to make war on us," said the fox. "Would you be able to help us?"

"Of course," replied the lynx. "I alone will defeat the bear, then I will drive him off." That was that. They set out together. But the lynx limped and lurched as he walked.

Soon, they met a skunk. "Are you a good fighter?" asked the fox.

"Of course!"

"How do you fight?"

The skunk turned around and demonstrated. "That is how I fight. I would drive away anyone, no matter who."

"A bear is going to fight us," said the fox. "You included. Will you help us?"

So off the three of them went until they met a porcupine. "Would you fight?" asked the fox.

"I'd rather not," replied the porcupine. "Nevertheless, if I did, no one would bother me. Whenever I'm cornered, I just roll up in a ball and whip my tail. I can drive away anyone."

"That'll be fine," said the fox. "Let's go."
And they left.

"You should really go on ahead," the fox said to the lynx.

So away they went in search of the bear. First was the lynx, followed by the skunk, and after that the porcupine. Last was the fox.

Now where the bear himself had gone, he saw

the wolf. "Okay!" said the bear, "I'm ready for that old fox." The wolf agreed to help him. "I have a grudge against him too," said the wolf.

As they went on their way, they met a rattlesnake. "Would you come along too?" asked the bear. "We are going to make war on this fox."

The sound of all of this pleased the snake. "Now," said the bear. "I will climb up over there, I will watch. Snake, you will lie in wait over there. Wolf, you will hide behind just over yonder. When they are about to arrive, you will strike the one who leads. As for myself, I will come down. Understood?"

By this time, the others were nearly there. From his lookout, the bear was first to see them. "Hey! Here they come!" he shouted.

"How many are there?" one of them asked. "What do they look like?" asked another.

"Well," said the bear, "the warrior who is leading is picking up rocks. It is hard to guess, but his bag must be very full. This other warrior, his war club is unbelievable: it is black and also white. As for this other one, I don't quite recognize this other warrior, but it's hard to imagine the number of arrows that he is carrying. Ah, and last, that old fox. Get everything ready!"

As soon as he heard that one of the warriors carried a stick, the snake made his way to a hole and disappeared down it. The wolf was afraid when he heard that another carried stones.

When the lynx, skunk, porcupine, and fox finally appeared over the rise, the rattlesnake gasped for want of air. His tail gave off a very faint "ch, ch, ch, ch, ch." Believing the rattle to be a signal, the wolf decided to attack. He burst out from his ambush, but as he did he collided with the lynx, who mauled him. The wolf began to howl.

The bear lumbered down from his perch, but because he was coming down backwards, he wasn't quite sure where he was going. The porcupine, who was climbing a tree, collided with the bear.

Hiyauh! It was indescribable! There was only one thing to do. He ran away, as did the other wild animals in every direction.

That was the last time that the animals ever fought.

"Dog! Bring Me a Beaver!"

"*Animoosh! Amik Abeedimoowishin!*"

Told by Basil H. Johnston

Translated from the Anishinaubae by Basil H. Johnston

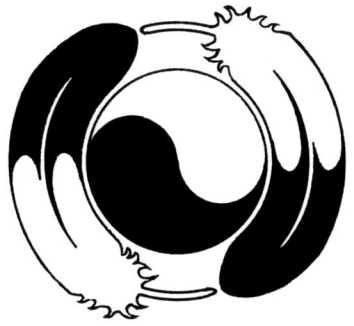

A certain old woman had a dog. Now, it was said that this dog had the ability to speak. Moreover, he understood humans.

The old lady lived alone. It's supposed, then, that she talked to her dog. He understood remarkably well.

Every morning, by force of habit, the dog went hunting. He brought back all kinds of meat—moose, deer, mink—all kinds of things—fish, birds. She was never hungry, this old woman.

The Anishinaubaek knew about this talking dog. From time to time they would come to visit him. But the dog would simply lie there, unspeaking. They spoke to him, but he would never reply. It also proved useless to offer him food. He could not be tempted in the slightest.

One day, the old woman remarked to her dog: "I have a powerful craving for beaver!" That is all she said. But she drew no attention whatever from that little dog; he was asleep.

When one week had passed she again spoke to him: "I really crave beaver; it's been so long since I've eaten one." But the dog paid no attention.

Some more time passed and the old woman spoke to the dog again: "Listen up, dog! Get me a beaver! I crave one in the worst way. It's been ten years since I ate one. You really don't need to go very far, just to the lake over there." Again the dog was not interested.

A little while later the old woman demanded again: "Did you not hear me? I said get me a beaver! I crave one endlessly. I'm tired of eating moose, deer, and trout. I need a beaver, I tell you! Now get to it!" But once again the dog ignored her.

Infuriated, the old lady fetched a stick and showed it to the dog: "See this! I'm telling you for the last time. Get me a beaver!!!" But the dog only looked at it with half-open eyes.

Ignored again, she began to thrash him. She beat him until he ran out of the house. Then he turned and spoke to her: "Watch out! Take care!"

"Don't bother me," she replied. "Away with you."

It was not long before the old dog dragged home a—what-do-you-call-it?—a beaver.

The old woman was said to have been singing cheerfully as she skinned this—thing—the beaver. The dog, for his part, only said, "Watch out! Take care!"

"For goodness sake," said the old lady, "leave me be."

When she finished cooking the beaver, how she enjoyed eating it. And as she ate, she threw little bones to the dog.

"For your own good, take care," he cautioned her.

The more she ate, the better the old woman enjoyed her food. She ate quickly. In a little while a small bone lodged in her throat. She screamed and screamed. "Oh, please help me," she begged. "Something is happening to me!" What was going on in that old lady's mind is anyone's guess.

"I told you so," said the dog. "I told you so."

Mermaids
Nebaunaubaequaen

Told by Sam Ozawamik

Collected and translated from the Anishinaubae
by Basil H. Johnston

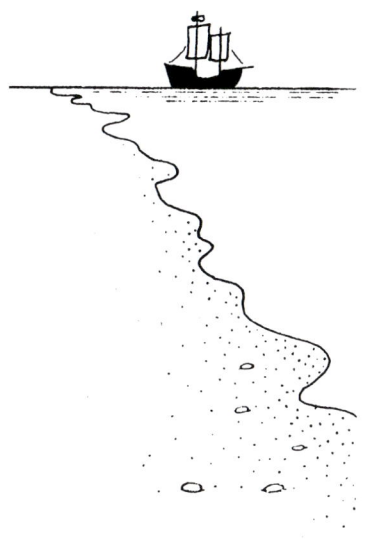

It is very old, this story. It concerns those who came to work. It was at Little Wikwemikong that they were to have disembarked. In commemoration of something, the Anishinaubaek drummed, near the far shore. For some reason they prayed, it is assumed.

They built a small church on the far shore. Its bell shone very brightly. It is uncertain where they had got it.

There was a bishop who used to pass through there. In the distance, but barely in view, was some object. It twinkled like a star. "What is that?" they asked.

One time, they say, the bishop passed through the waters there. "I would like to take a brief look at that church," he said to the ship's captain. "Let us stop there for a while." Forthwith, the captain changed the ship's course. It was a large vessel, according to accounts.

That was the first time that the Anishinaubaek saw them. Without doubt, they were afraid. They fled, somewhere to the States. That was supposed to be the time that they saw a boat change course. That is how he described it, he who told me.

At once, it is said, an old woman ran about. She was decidedly making a din: "Go back! Go back!" she was reported to have said. "Soldiers are arriving," she shouted everywhere. The old woman created an uproar. They all fled inland — women, children, everyone who was there.

The priest saw the commotion on the shore and decided not to disembark.

Everyone had fled inland. "We are going to be taken or killed," they probably thought. That is why they fled inland. Only later did they realize what had happened. The priest himself might have told this story.

It was known as "Old Town." The bay was long. There was also a small lake situated there.

The place where the waters flowed, where the boats came in, was narrow. That is where the Anishinaubaek camped. It was then that they saw the mermaids for the first time.

The mermaids helped the Anishinaubaek. It got to be impossible for the Anishinaubaek to go anywhere without the mermaids following. It was at night that they appeared.

Thunderbirds
Nimkii-Bineshiinyag

Told by Jonas George *(Wah-sa-ghe-zik)*
Rama First Nation, 1916

 One man was newly married and was out hunting in the bush, trying to catch some game. It was in the fall hunting, and he camped there all fall till the lake froze up. He hunted beaver through the ice. He cut holes through the ice to find the hole in the ground where the beaver went in. (Bank beaver who live in holes in the banks of lakes and rivers.) He hunted with a dog.

This man's father heard rumours. Trouble might come at night on the ice. Might be something come on you or happen to you, so the man went to go home after dark and crossed the ice, about two hundred yards across. There was little moonlight. He got about half way over, and for just a moment he could see the moon. Something just like a dark cloud came over the moon and he heard something over his head which came down (this was a big monster eagle with wings about twenty feet long and body about eight feet wide). So this Thunderbird caught the man in its claws and took him up in the sky, and the man never knew anything for a long time, and was taken right over the clouds.

This man began to wake up, inside the bird's claws. He has his pole (ice chisel) in his hand yet, what he used to cut through the ice with in hunting for beaver. This man is big and heavy. The eagle

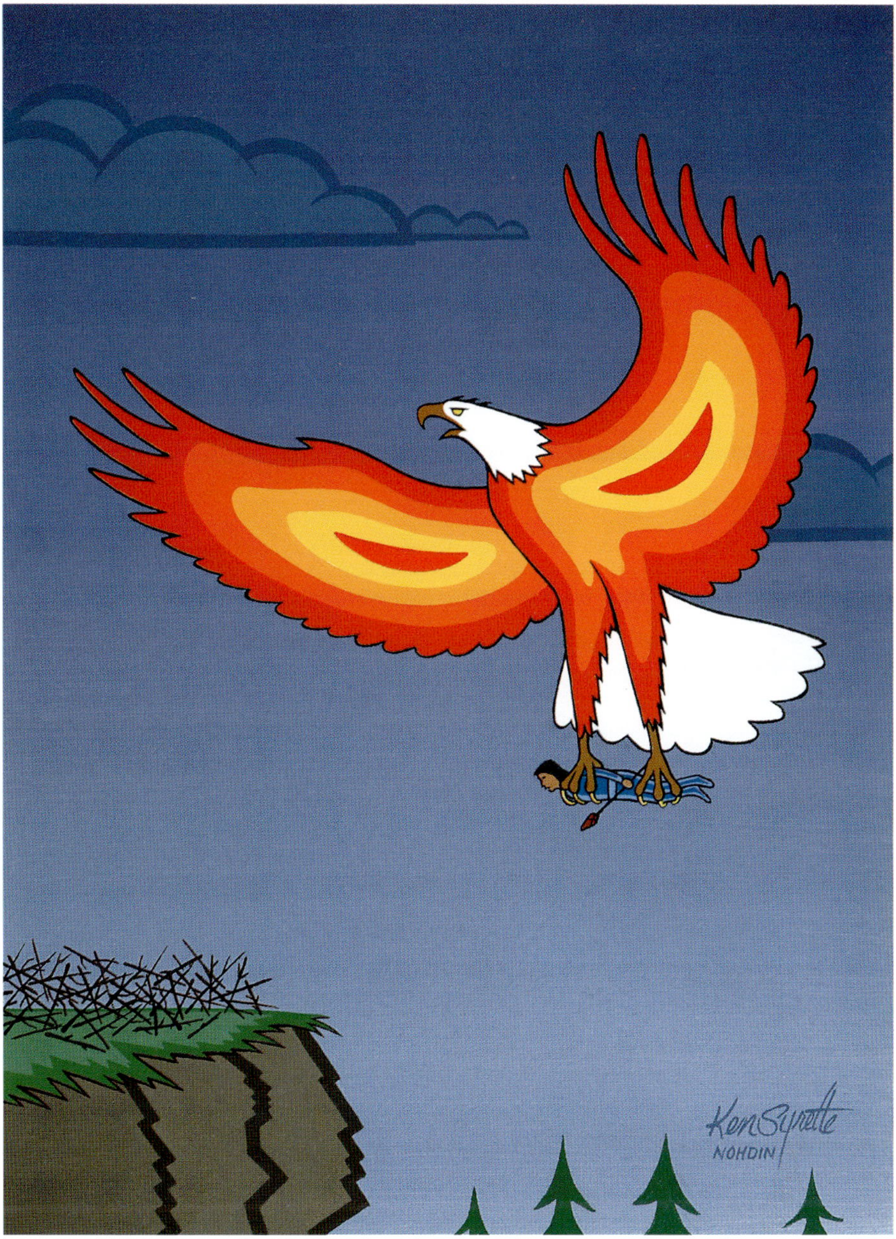
Ken Syrette
NOHDIN

had long claws, about twelve inches long, lots of room for the man to lay in them. This man looks up and sees a rock were the eagle goes to, a big bluff and a very high place. The eagle takes a rest on top. The eagle lets the man go. The man looks around and sees some young eagles sitting down. The man looks at the young birds who are moving all the time towards him. The man began to be afraid of them.

The old eagle took the man for food. The man had the pole in his hand and walks towards the young birds and hit one of them and killed it, rolled it to the edge of the rock, opened the belly, took all the insides out, and went in himself. He had string to close up the opening by sewing. The man began moving and the bird fell down off the rock. He can't tell where he goes down for a long time. He can't see anything for a long while. And when he didn't feel any moving (movement) he began to cut the string and got out and looked around.

He was standing on the ice on the shore of a lake, so he went on. He goes very far and came across a snowshoe track. He went on and came to a house where someone was living. He saw an old man and woman. These people spoke and asked him if he was hungry, so he got something to eat. It was nice, and he stayed with them for a long while.

The old man went out every day and came back after sundown, and the woman went out every night and came back just at daylight. One time the old man spoke and said, "I take you home tomorrow morning." This man got on the old man's back, who walked very fast. The old man spoke, "You look out if you see any track on the snow." He looked and saw old tracks and the old man dropped him down.

This man went on. Travelled long distance. He came to a long, narrow place and stood and looked around. The place was almost like where he was in the first place when the eagle took him.

This man began to know quite well where he had camped. He went a little way and began to know that he was at his landing. He saw a woman coming to the shore, an old grey-headed woman. That was his wife. He had been away for years, and his wife was very old. I think he is living there yet.

Thunder/Monsters

Nim-Mah-Kie/ Miisaandamoog

Told by Jonas George *(Wah-sa-ghe-zik)*
Rama First Nation, 1914

Many years ago, a man went into the woods to hunt. It came on a storm and he took a line for camp. It came on worse, and he crawled under a projecting pine tree. He saw the lightning strike several trees, and looking very closely at one of them, he saw a little man, and looking again at the tree, he saw another.

Both these men were fine little fellows, all black and shining, and are called *Nim-Mah-Kie* (thunder). They climbed up in the air as if they were climbing ladders, and disappeared. After that, more lightning came down. These little men set the lightning at the trees and make the thunder. Thunder and lightning keep the monsters down on the land and in the lakes.

These monsters live in hills near lakes. They have underground passages to the water, and can sometimes be seen early in the morning.

One of these monsters lives in the hill just north of where the old Indian portage from Lake Simcoe enters West Bay, Balsam Lake. Another lives in the hill at Atherley, Rama Reserve, Lake Couchiching, and another lives up north in a lake whose name is now forgotten.

Thunder and lightning kill these monsters.

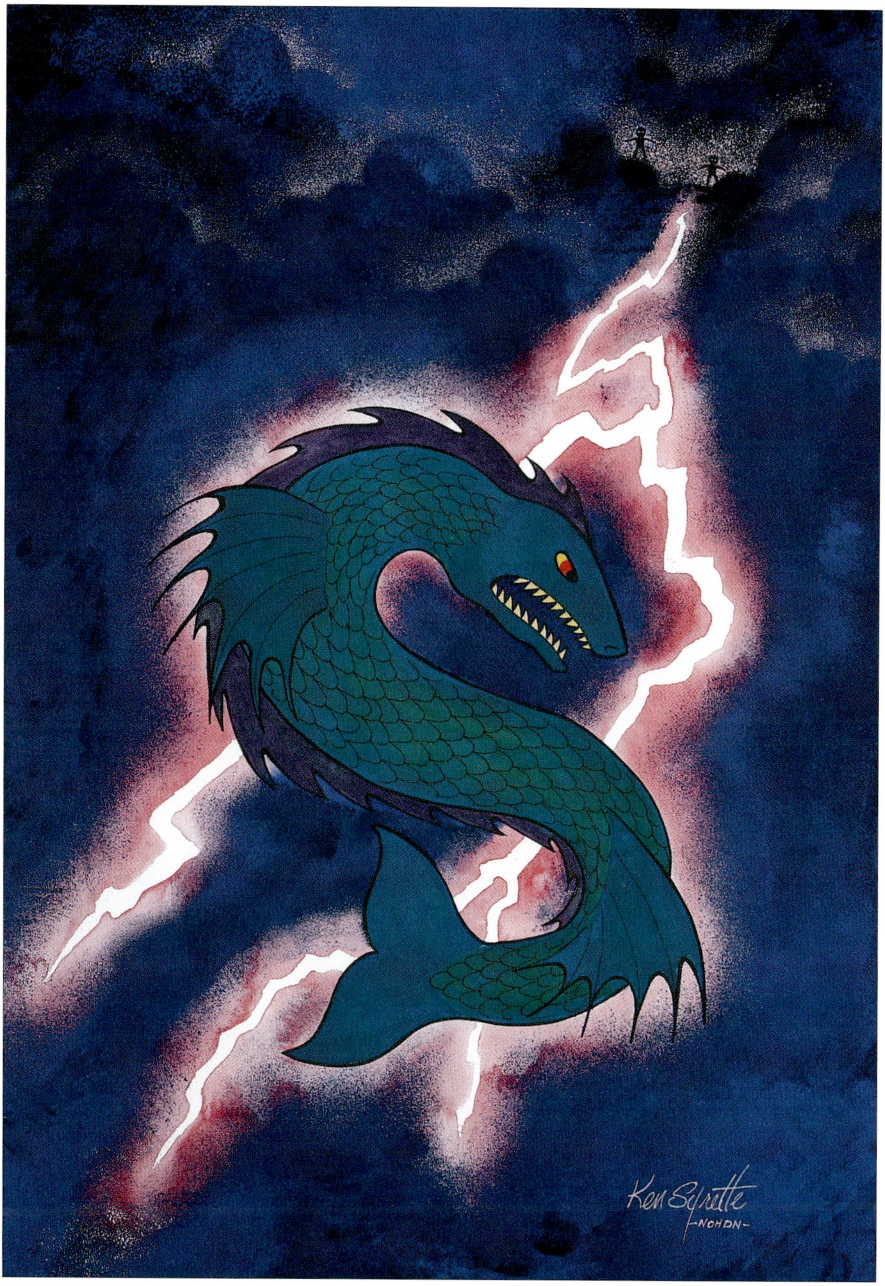
Ken Syrette
-NOHDN-

What the Dog Did

Animoosh w'gauh izhitchigaet

Told by Frank Shawbedees

Collected and translated from the Anishinaubae
by Basil H. Johnston

A long time ago, all the animals spoke to one another. Without exception, they understood each other. They also understood the Anishinaubaek, just as the Anishinaubaek understood the animals.

As time passed, the Anishinaubaek found life increasingly difficult. "Aha! We must go out hunting," they began to say. "Well, then," one of them announced, "this is the one that you will hunt." To another he said, "You! Seek out the bear in order to kill him." To others still he announced: "A deer for you; a duck for you; a wolf for you." This leader assigned an animal to each of them. Soon enough, the Anishinaubaek were killing the wild animals.

The animals were offended. So they all came together and spoke. They held a council. "Why is it that the Anishinaubaek are always killing us?" one of them asked.

"Only that they themselves might live," replied another.

"Some of us are becoming fewer," remarked another. "There is not a sufficient number among some of us. Take for example the deer. The Anishinaubaek have killed them nearly into extinction. The Anishinaubaek ought not to kill the deer now; later, when they are more numerous."

Another spoke to the wolf. "You are killed by them, and you kill only the sick of the wild animals in order to survive. When you see an Anishinaubae you will yell, howl, to let us know that he is approaching."

He spoke also to the bear: "Bear, you too are becoming fewer in number. Yes, indeed. No longer simply wait when the Anishinaubae comes, go and hide. We are too few in number.

"And you, Beaver," he said, "when you see an Anishinaubae coming along, strike the water so that we will know when he is near. Birds, also, cry out only when the Anishinaubae draws near."

The dog sat there, saying nothing but listening to everything.

"Aha!" he thought to himself,

"I will help the Anishinaubae.

I will go tell him."

The animals adjourned their council. The birds flew off in all directions. The ducks took flight. The bear, the beaver, the wolf, the fox—all of them left. The dog himself left and went to visit the Anishinaubaek.

"Do you want to know something?" he said to them. "Today you're not going to find anyone when you go hunting."

"How is that?" asked one of the Anishinaubae.

"The animals held a meeting today, and that is what they decided. Apparently, there are too few of some of them; it seems that you are killing them all off in order for you to eat. So, I've come to tell you."

"And what do you want in return?"

"Oh, I'll tell you later."

With that, the dog left. It was indeed true that when the Anishinaubaek went hunting they found nothing. "What shall we do?" one of them asked. "We do not see a wild animal anywhere. Not a one. I hear them though. Some of them are wandering nearby. They are hidden."

Another spoke: "The reason why the wild animals were put here was so that we could eat. So that we could live! We must find them."

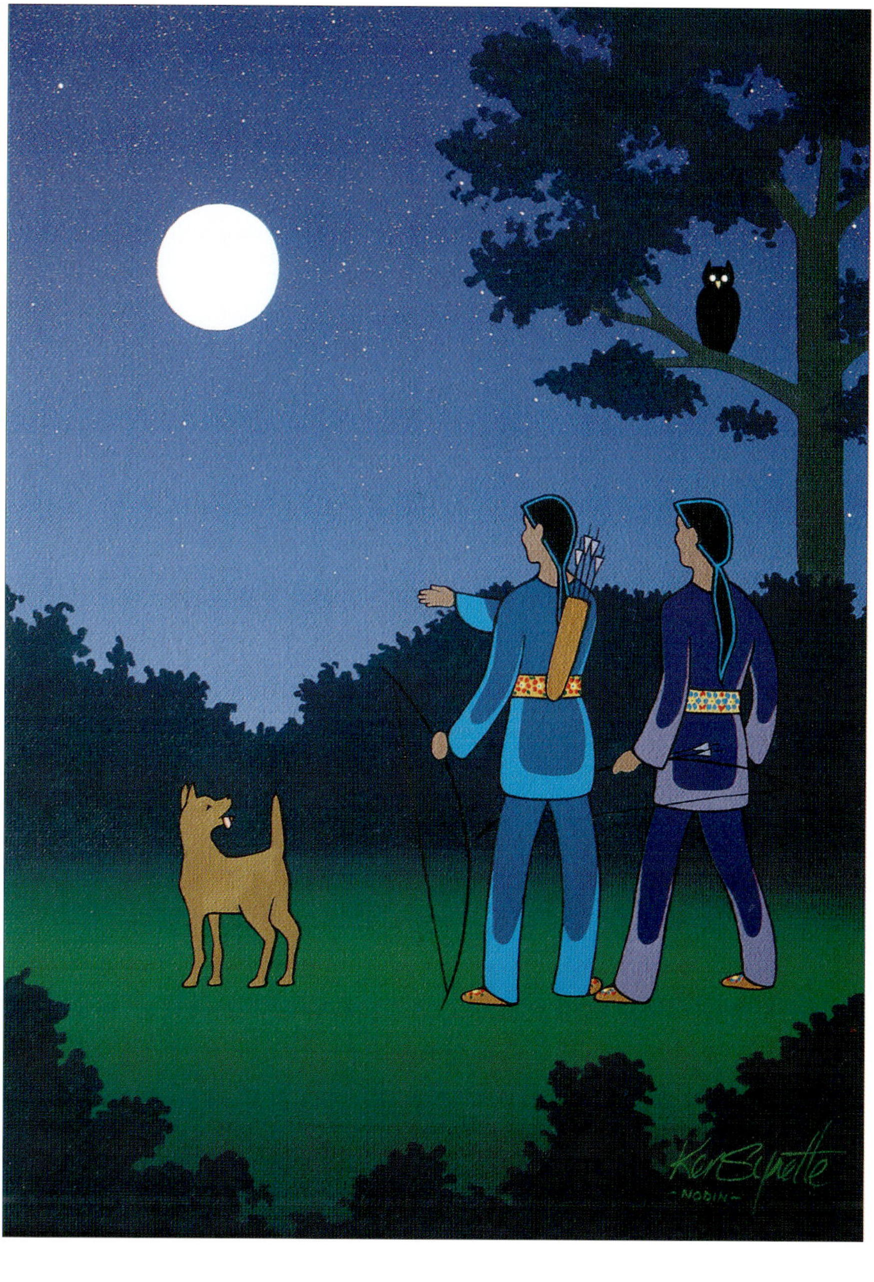
-NODIN-

In time, the animals held another council. The owl, who was their leader, spoke first. "I do not see quite so well during the day," he noted. "But it is unbelievable how well I see at night. The Anishinaubae is now doing things differently. He waits for us to sleep, and then he catches us. He kills us still. Someone is revealing something. Someone is reporting to him. Someone is helping the Anishinaubae. Otherwise, he would never find us where we go to sleep. Someone takes him there."

The dog sat. On and on. He said nothing.

The skunk observed this dog. He noted that the dog was listening carefully, but saying nothing. Eventually, the dog left, even before the animals had finished meeting.

The skunk decided to speak with the wolf. "Did you see that?" he asked. "The dog sneaked out of here while we were speaking."

"Tell the others," replied the wolf. "I will keep an eye on him to see where he might be going." With that, the wolf left.

As instructed, the skunk alerted everyone present.

Meanwhile, the dog ran directly to where the Anishinaubaek were. The wolf followed. He prowled nearby and was able to hear the dog in conversation with them. This is what the dog said: "You are killing too many of them in the places where I send you. Kill only one at a time, not two, not three. In that way no one will know much more."

"What do you want for helping us?" one of the Anishinaubaek again asked the dog.

As before, he would not commit: "I will tell you later, later," he commented.

The wolf set out at once upon hearing all of this. The wild animals were still meeting when he returned. "It is the dog who is helping the Anishinaubaek to kill us!" he announced. "It is the dog who leads them to us!"

At that point, the dog returned. "It is unlikely that they saw me leave," he thought. Quietly, he slipped back into his place.

"Ha!" remarked the owl. "We have here with us one who is killing us; he himself is not doing the killing, but he helps the Anishinaubaek to do so. Nevertheless, he is as responsible as if he had himself killed us."

"You, dog!" said the bear. "For what you are doing, no wild animal will ever again go to you.

From now on you will not be understood. No wild animal will understand you. Not even the Anishinaubae himself will understand you. Besides, you will lose your speech. When you come near, everyone will leave. For as long as you live, no one will approach you. Ever. Even if you try to talk to the Anishinaubae, he will not understand you; but you will understand him. Moreover, the Anishinaubae will not treat you well. He will feed you his scraps, what he leaves after eating. So long as you live, you will depend on the Anishinaubae to look after you. He will kick you, he will make you work. For as long as you live, for as long as this Earth may last, for as long as the Anishinaubaek exist, you, you will suffer. At some future date, when the Earth comes to an end, only then will you stop suffering."

And that is what happens today. The dog understands human beings. The wolf tries to kill the dog wherever he meets him. If the dog happens to wander about near the forest, the wild animals will go elsewhere. If the Anishinaubae has a dog, he makes him work. The dog carries burdens, he draws a sled—all kinds of things. And besides, whatever leftovers he may have, the Anishinaubae feeds the dog.

If the dog is in the way for any length of time, the Anishinaubae kicks him.

The Closed-Eyes Dance

Pizungowaubigauh

Told by Frank Shawbedees

Collected and translated from the Anishinaubae
by Basil H. Johnston

It was already well into autumn. Nanabush was sitting and sitting. Well, you know what Nanabush is like. He is somewhat foolish. He did all kinds of things to make life hard for the Anishinaubaek, and for the animals—and he was always hungry.

One morning he awoke and ate a little bit of meat. Then he was on his way to meddle with the Anishinaubaek, who were working. Ah! He came back. It was already mid-day. Yonder he went, still looking for something to eat. Nothing there. So he sat down. "I'm hungry," he said. "What should I do?" Then an idea came to him. "I know! I will ask the animals to come along, to come and eat. They won't suspect a thing."

So he travelled about, inviting the animals to his banquet. All except the skunk. When the animals arrived, Nanabush built a fire. The animals sat around it, as was to be expected.

"When exactly are we going to eat?" one of them asked.

Soon after, so did another: "When are we going to eat?"

"Oh," announced Nanabush. "First we'll have a good time. Let's play. We'll play first."

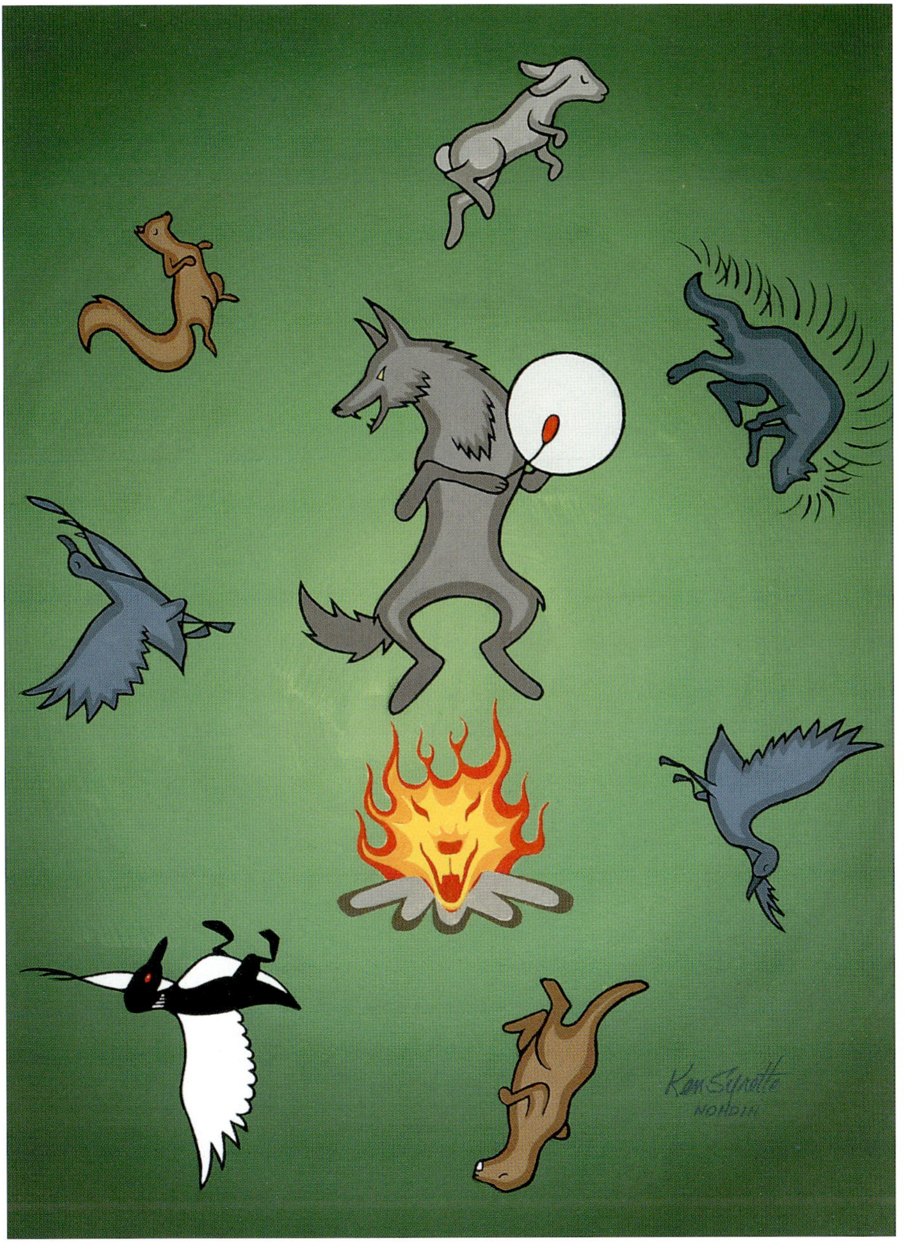
NOHDIH

So they played for a while, and then they sat down once more.

"When are we going to eat?" another of them asked.

"Oh," said Nanabush, "first we must dance. We must dance first."

For this, Nanabush sat down. Then he took up his drum and made music. "All of you must dance, every one of you," he said. "I will drum."

As they began to dance, he made an announcement: "You must also close your eyes. You have to close your eyes. That's all there is to it."

As they had been asked, they closed their eyes. As each one of the animals danced near him he felt its flesh.

"Hmm, not enough meat on this one. Nor on this." A squirrel came near, but he missed him. And then a duck came by. "Yes!" said Nanabush, "this is the one. I will wait for him to come around again."

When it did he twisted that duck's neck and broke it. Then he put the duck behind him, in a hiding place, in case someone was watching.

A loon came by next. He felt that too. The bird suspected something. "Something is happening here," he thought.

Another duck came by. The loon, who had one eye open, saw Nanabush squeeze the duck.

"Everything is fine," said Nanabush. The loon continued to dance. Soon, though, he opened his eye again and saw Nanabush throttling the duck.

"Watch out!" cried the loon. "This Nanabush is killing us. He invited us to eat, but he is eating us!"

Everyone ran, no one excepted. All of them ran from there, in every direction.

Nanabush jumped to his feet and tried to catch the birds he wanted to eat. As he ran, he stepped on the beaver's tail. Now, until that time the beaver's tail was round, but Nanabush flattened it with his weight. That is why the beaver's tail is flat today.

As it happened, the loon was the last of the animals out of there. "This is terrible," Nanabush growled, and he gave the loon a hard kick in the rump. It is for this reason that the loon's legs are situated so far to the back of its body.

Nanabush was often foolish, to be sure.

The Star-Man

Nangiiwnini

Told by Jonas George *(Wah-sa-ghe-zik)*

Rama First Nation, 1916

This happened a long time ago, about four hundred years ago maybe. There were five or six hundred who were living together on what is now called Pine Plains. They had a big time there.

One day, two of them walked up and looked around the plains. At a little distance they saw someone sitting on the grass. This was a man, so they went to see. When he put up his hand to keep them back, they stopped and looked. After a while, he spoke: "I don't belong to this land; I dropped from above, yesterday, so I am here now." The men invited the star-man to the place where they lived. "Yes," he said, "you go home and clean the place where I will stay, and come back again, then I will go with you in a few days."

The men went home and told the people about it. They began to clean the place where they were to keep the star-man for two days. Then they went to get him.

Star-Man was a good-looking man, clean and shining bright. At sundown, he looked up to the skies, as if he were watching for something. Just after dark he spoke: "In two days, I will return to the sky. Something will come down to take me there."

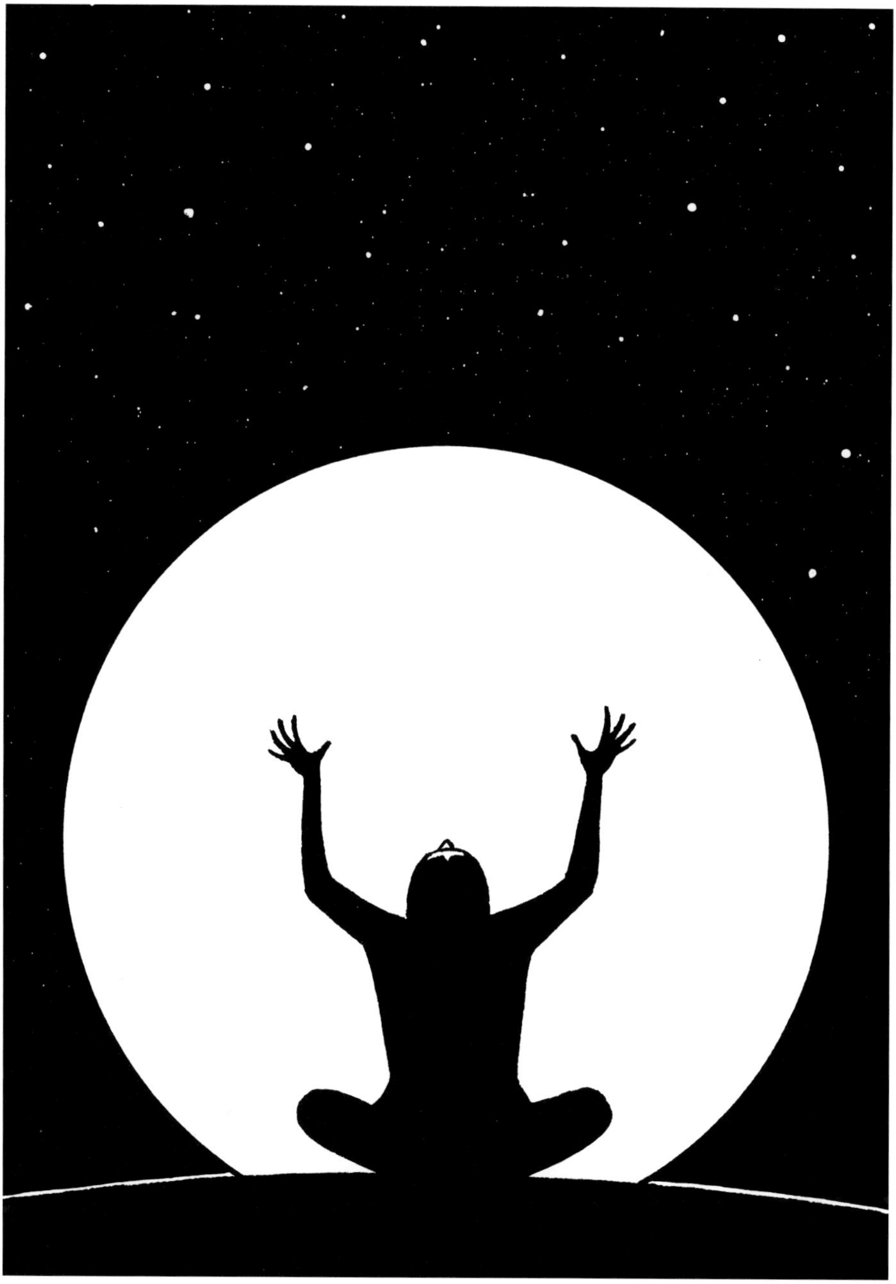

He told them that where he came from he was running. There was an open place and he couldn't stop running; so he got in and dropped down. The next day he said that it was a good country where he lived, that everything was good. "Tomorrow at midnight, I will return to the stars," he said. "All of you must be home to watch me leave."

Just after midnight the next day, he looked up and said, "It's coming." Everyone looked up but could see nothing for a long time. The man who had kept the star-man at his home could see well, and saw something like a bright star shining high up. The other people couldn't see anything until it came near the ground. This was the most beautiful thing ever seen in this world. Two men got hold of it and pulled down hard. The star-man entered into it, and it rose into the sky.

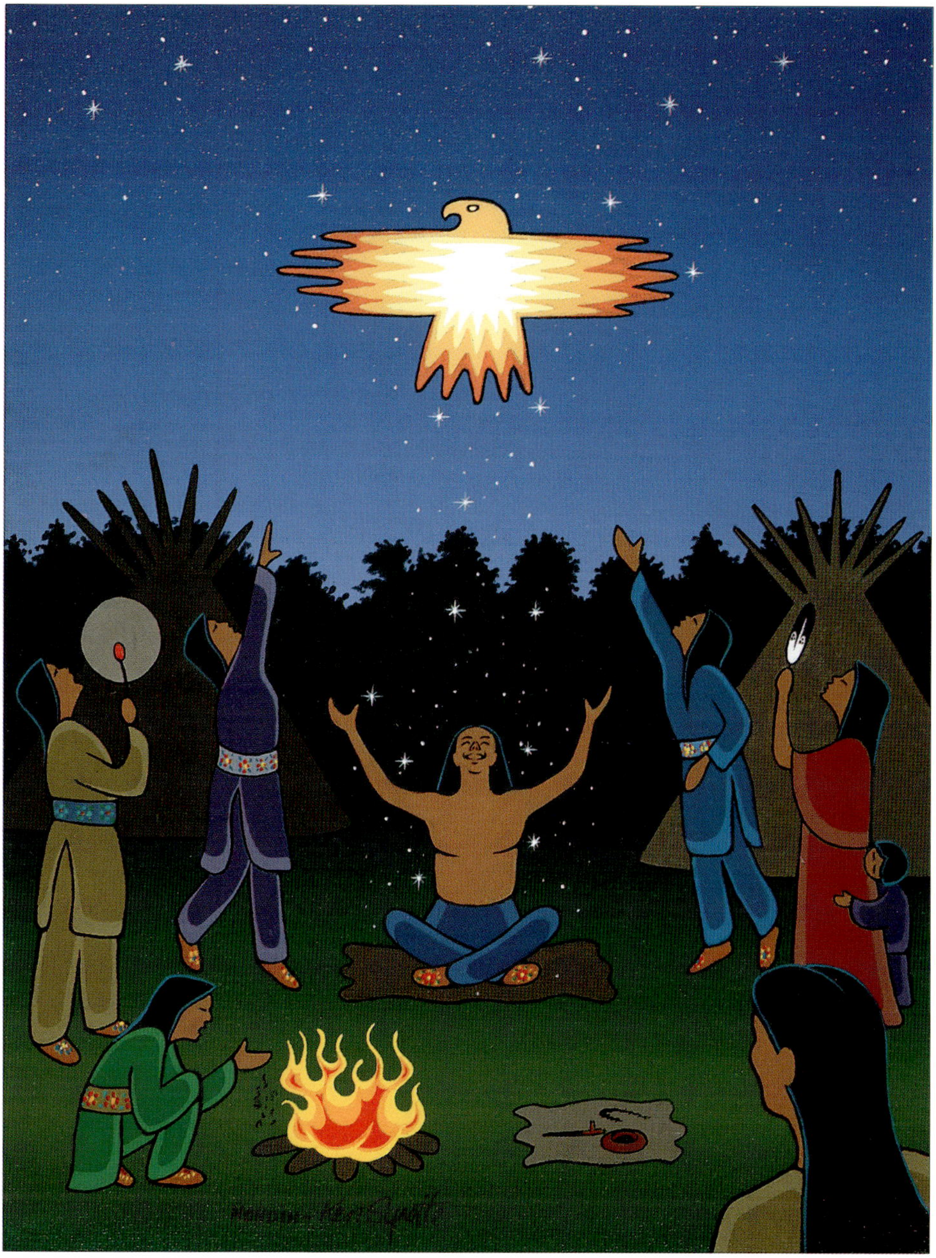